MINDFULNESS FOR LITTLE ONES

MINDFULNESS
for LITTLE ONES

Playful Activities to Foster
Empathy, Self-Awareness, and Joy in Kids

Hiedi France, EdD

Illustrations by Denise Holmes

ROCKRIDGE
PRESS

Art Director: Jennifer Hsu
Art Producer: Hannah Dickerson
Editor: Clara Song Lee
Production Editor: Ashley Polikoff
Illustrations © 2020 Denise Holmes
Author photo courtesy of Alicia's Photography

ISBN: Print 978-1-64611-882-3 | eBook 978-1-64611-883-0

R0

THIS WORK IS DEDICATED TO MY FAMILY, WHO HAS FILLED MY LIFE WITH INSPIRATION AND PURPOSE: MY SON, WHO TEACHES ME MORE THAN ANY BOOK COULD; MY DAUGHTER, WHO REMINDS ME TO BE THE BEST VERSION OF MYSELF; AND MY HUSBAND, WHO SUPPORTS ALL MY AMBITIONS. I LOVE YOU!

CONTENTS

INTRODUCTION

WE ARE SHAPED BY OUR THOUGHTS; WE BECOME
WHAT WE THINK. WHEN THE MIND IS PURE,
JOY FOLLOWS LIKE A SHADOW THAT NEVER LEAVES.

—BUDDHA

I am so glad you are here! If you're reading this book, it's probably safe to say that you have an interest in mindfulness. Whether it's simply a curiosity or something you have practiced on your own and now want to introduce to your children, I embrace you in a warm hug. You are valued, just as you are.

In his book *Wherever You Go, There You Are,* Jon Kabat-Zinn describes mindfulness as "paying attention in a particular way: on purpose, in the present moment, and nonjudgmentally." Practicing this in everyday life is the ultimate challenge and goal. Mindfulness is a way of being, seeing, and experiencing all that humanity has to offer. Life will undoubtably throw many challenges at you, and the practice of mindfulness can change the way you tackle them.

My journey to mindfulness has been a slow awakening. I wish I had this book when my children were toddlers and preschoolers. While I have always parented with love and peace, I would have loved to have a greater awareness of how mindful activities could have supported

my kids through the younger years. As the parent of a son with ADHD, I have learned how teaching children to understand their emotions can lead to feelings of calm, peace, and joy. And my work with special needs students has helped me develop activities that support mindfulness at even the earliest of ages.

My hope is that the activities in this book will help you on your journey in introducing mindfulness to your little one. Nothing in this book is grand or groundbreaking—it is simply a new way to approach and complete activities that support your little ones as they grow and experience the wonders of life. Have fun as you try them out! If you or your little ones don't like a few, that's okay. In fact, you can modify any of the activities so that they're more meaningful to you or your child. As long as you're spending even brief moments of time paying attention to the present moment together, then you are succeeding in planting seeds of mindfulness in your little ones' hearts, and they will blossom with self-awareness, love, and joy.

1

Mindfulness for Little Ones

Caring for a toddler or preschooler can bring much joy—and it can also be super stressful at times. Young children are learning about boundaries (and testing them), while also figuring out how to communicate their wants and needs. One of the ways adults can help little ones succeed is to build mindfulness practices that foster nonjudgmental love and acceptance of what's happening in the present moment—a strength that will help children learn to pause and respond to challenges more skillfully as they get older.

Planting Seeds of Mindfulness

Mindfulness is a practice of being fully present, aware of our surroundings, and not overreacting or getting overwhelmed by what's going on around us. That might seem impossible for children ages two to five, but trust me, this is actually the perfect age to plant the seeds of mindfulness. Young children can be taught mindfulness using toys, through focused movement of their body, and by listening carefully to sounds. These practices can provide the foundation of skills that will help them focus attention and regulate emotions as they grow. The skills needed include:

* **Mindful breathing.** Teaching children the importance of their breath helps them learn how to center the brain and body. This skill can be learned through activities such as imitating certain animals and using toys to support full and deep breathing.

* **Self-awareness.** Young children are often overly focused on what they want or need, and mindfulness can help them put those feelings into words, instead of crying or throwing tantrums.

* **Mindful movement.** It's no secret that little ones like to move around. And they can use that movement to be mindful about themselves and their world.

What Mindfulness Won't Do

Mindfulness is the practice of being present exactly where you are without judgment—it is not about controlling thoughts and feelings. Instead, it teaches us how to realize that certain thoughts and feelings are present, and then accept them without judging ourselves for having them. Often, this brief moment of recognition is enough to allow a person to respond more skillfully to challenging thoughts and feelings instead of reacting impulsively. So, although practicing mindfulness with your young child may not reduce tantrums or strong reactions, over time it can help you and your child feel less out of control when experiencing difficult emotions. Then, when a tantrum does occur, it becomes an opportunity to breathe through it and learn from it rather than view it as something that has to be stopped and controlled.

Helping Mindfulness Sprout

Young children ages two to five are busy learners. They are curious by nature and avid explorers. The activities in this book harness those strengths by presenting everyday items in new ways. In addition, the activities are fast, easy to complete, and meant to be repeated over and over.

One thing to remember as you work your way through the book is that these activities are meant to be fun and engaging. Stay in the moment. If the activity calls for glitter but your child really wants to use uncooked pasta, celebrate their sense of creativity. Young children also have limited attention spans—usually two to five minutes per year of life. The activities in this book have been designed with that in mind.

Two-Year-Olds

Believe it or not, the terrible twos don't need to be so terrible. Toddlers love to explore their environment, which means they really shouldn't be expected to sit still for long periods of time. And while they are able to say simple two- to four-word sentences to communicate their wants and needs, they will still need plenty of help in learning how to relay their feelings and stay calm when things don't go their way.

CAPABILITIES AND LIMITATIONS

* **Attention span.** Two-year-olds have an attention span that lasts about 4 to 10 minutes. They can follow simple instructions and enjoy activities that include hands-on materials. Little ones in this age group enjoy repetition, so activities should be predictable.

* **Language/communication.** While their language is growing, two-year-olds still use their behavior to communicate many of their emotions and needs.

* **Social/emotional.** Most toddlers can identify key body parts and point to them on themselves or others. However, they cannot fully express feelings or read facial expressions. Solitary play is still key, but they are starting to notice other children and play beside them. Just remember that these little ones lack the capability to understand how others feel, or to change their actions based on other people's feelings.

THE MINDFUL TWO-YEAR-OLD

Mindful toddlers can complete basic breathing exercises and explore their body and facial expressions. They love using hands-on exploration and can easily engage in any of the activities that include movement and visual prompts. Two-year-olds are also mostly concerned with the present and tend to respond automatically to how they feel.

Three-Year-Olds

This is usually the age when children are starting preschool and becoming much more independent. They can often separate from primary caregivers without much stress. They are also beginning to become much more aware of other people around them and that these individuals have their own emotions. Three-year-olds can say their names, beginning the process of identity formation.

CAPABILITIES AND LIMITATIONS

* **Attention span.** Preschoolers have an attention span of about 6 to 15 minutes. They can follow two- or three-step instructions and are beginning to understand concepts like *in*, *on*, and *under*. They still enjoy hands-on activities that include movement and play.

* **Language/Communication.** Three-year-olds are beginning to understand pronouns like *I*, *me*, *we*, and *you*. They can carry on a conversation using two or three sentences. Yet, even with increased language, they may still struggle to express needs with words when they're upset.

* **Social/emotional.** These little ones are beginning to play *with* friends, instead of just next to them, and they can even take turns in games. Three-year-olds can express a wide range of emotions, show concern for others, and identify feelings in books.

THE MINDFUL THREE-YEAR-OLD

At this age, kids can sit for longer periods of time, so they can start to recognize their breathing and become more aware of their bodies and personal space. Three-year-olds can be taught how to show kindness and care for others through thoughts and actions, and they can identify how they are feeling. However, they may still have a hard time putting their feelings into words.

Four-Year-Olds

As children at this age enter the exciting environment of pre-kindergarten, their world is expanding more and more. And they are ready for it! Four-year-olds are open to trying new things and enjoy playing with other children more than by themselves. They love pretend play and can get super creative when it comes to story lines and characters. The four-year-old brain is also beginning to focus on the refinement of fine motor skills, which allows them to start learning tasks such as writing, cutting, and manipulating smaller games and puzzle pieces.

CAPABILITIES AND LIMITATIONS

* **Attention span.** Four-year-olds typically have an attention span of 8 to 20 minutes, so they can listen to longer stories in books and begin to predict what might happen next. They can also sing songs and retell stories from memory.

* **Language/communication.** Children of this age love to ask lots of questions. They have a basic understanding of how things are the same and different, and they're also beginning to understand pronouns like *he*, *she*, and *they*, which can lead to a deeper understanding of different gender identities.

* **Social/emotional.** Four-year-olds have a greater ability to tell you what they like and need, and can pick from choices with two or three options. They are also learning how to problem-solve with friends but will still need help in managing these complex interactions.

THE MINDFUL FOUR-YEAR-OLD

Four-year-olds have a much better understanding of what they can do to bring awareness to the present, including sitting and looking around their environment without having to touch items. They can also use their imagination when describing things not present and predict how things could make them feel. But just like their younger peers, they still need direct teaching to understand different role-playing situations.

Five-Year-Olds

At age five, children are starting (or will soon start) kindergarten. They are better at self-control and purposeful behavior, but they can still have meltdowns and struggle to regulate emotions. Even so, they do want to please adults and friends, which allows them to follow more set routines and tasks.

CAPABILITIES AND LIMITATIONS

* **Attention span.** Five-year-olds typically have an attention span of 10 to 25 minutes. This allows the connections in their brain to strengthen for repeated tasks and leads to deeper understanding of the world around them.

* **Language/communication.** Children at this age can express their wants and needs clearly. However, they often have a hard time understanding when a request can be honored and when it cannot, which can lead to meltdowns when they don't get their way.

* **Social/emotional.** As they start their elementary school years, five-year-olds are ready to build more friendships and participate in play groups away from their primary caregivers. While they can work on simple problems with friends, they still need help to handle conflicts.

THE MINDFUL FIVE-YEAR-OLD

Five-year-olds can sit still for longer periods of time, as well as work to calm their body and brain when given the right tools. They can also focus on short-term goals to get something they want or to plan for a future event.

Every Child Is Beautifully Different

Every child develops differently and at their own pace—and all of the activities in this book can be easily adapted for any child. If you are working with a specialist, be sure to ask them for help in making any necessary changes so that your little one can still benefit from the tasks in the book.

* **Developmental delays.** If your child has weaknesses in one or more area, you can help them build confidence by using their strengths. For example, if your child is struggling with expressive language, use visuals to support their speech. Instead of asking them to say how they feel, print a feelings chart (these can easily be found online) and have them point to the word that corresponds to their emotion.

* **Autism spectrum disorder.** Children with this diagnosis can have many delays that impact their ability to cope with everyday tasks. They can experience behavior concerns due to issues with processing sights, scents, noises, or textures. Mindfulness can be a great way to help introduce your child to experiences in a loving and supportive way. However, do not force your child to complete activities that will overwhelm them. For example, if you are exploring nature with bare feet, and your child does not like the feel of grass, have them wear socks or use their hands instead.

* **Cognitive or physical disabilities.** Children with cognitive or physical disabilities may need support to complete some of the activities. Even if they require extra help, exploring the environment through their senses can help strengthen multiple pathways in their brain.

The Grown-Up Guide to Modeling Mindfulness

No matter your personal experience, one way you can support your young child in building mindfulness is to model it for them by naming body sensations, thoughts, and emotions when you are together. The more your child hears how the world impacts *you*, the easier it will be for them to bring awareness to their own experiences. For example, when enjoying playtime with your child you could say, "My heart feels full and happy when we are playing together."

Also, when doing the activities in this book together, don't forget to talk about how they make each of you feel. It is okay if you or your child do not like a particular activity. Mindfulness is about embracing all experiences—the good and the not-so-good.

Supporting Little Ones through Co-Regulation

As little ones grow and experience more of the world around them, there is an increased need for them to become better at regulating their thoughts, feelings, and behaviors. One way to foster this growth is through co-regulation. In the book *Self-Regulation and Toxic Stress: Foundations for Understanding Self-Regulation from an Applied Developmental Perspective*, the authors define co-regulation as warm and responsive interactions that provide the support children need to "understand, express, and modulate their thoughts, feelings, and behaviors." In order to achieve this, caregivers will need to pay close attention to the child's cues and respond consistently and sensitively with support.

Young children need consistent guidance from their caregivers to learn how to cope with their expanding world. For example, if your child is putting together a puzzle and you see them slamming the pieces in frustration, you can say, "I see that you are frustrated with the puzzle. Do you need help?" Bringing awareness to their emotions helps them understand that their feelings aren't good or bad. Instead, emotions are something that can be handled with external supports or internal resources.

Finally, remember to model for your child how *you* handle emotions. When completing a difficult task, you can say, "Wow, I am really frustrated right now. I think I am going to take a few deep breaths and see if I can come up with a better way to solve this." Modeling how you regulate your emotions helps your child see that everyone experiences emotions (even their parents!), and they can be handled in a safe way.

SAFETY TIPS

～～～

The activities in this book help foster mindfulness through exploration of the self and the world. However, caregivers should remember that young children need supervision with most of the activities. A few safety tips to keep in mind:

* Small items can become a choking hazard. Be sure to supervise children when creating with beads, pasta, balloons, and other small items. If an item becomes loose, be sure to remove or secure it immediately.

* Use child-friendly paints and glues, which can be found in most craft stores.

* When creating sensory bottles, use a permanent glue to secure the lid. Allow the glue to dry completely and test that it can't be opened before giving it to your child.

* Supervise young children when outside at all times.

How to Use This Book

This book is divided into five types of mindfulness activities that are appropriate for children ages two to five: Dance, Wiggle, and Move; Fun with the Five Senses; Adventures in Feelings; I Care, You Care, We Care; and Winding Down Time.

Due to their limited attention spans and capabilities, most activities are designed to be quick and require few materials and little prep time. Keep your child's capabilities in mind when choosing which activities to do and how many you can tackle each day. Most young children love repeating activities, and repetition helps them create good mindfulness habits.

Within each area, the activities are ordered from simple to complex, with a list of materials and how much prep time will be needed. Most activities can be modified so that they can be used with multiple ages, and each comes with a messiness rating from 0 (no cleanup needed) to 3 (more than 15 minutes of cleanup).

As a bonus, each activity includes one of the following four types of tips: an "age adaptation" tip to adjust the activity for different age ranges; a "simple swap" tip for material alternatives; a "get creative" tip to expand the activity using different settings or materials; or a "co-regulation" tip for how you can engage with the activity to support your child.

2

Dance, Wiggle, and Move

We don't need to sit still to be mindful. In fact, young children learn and grow when they get to move around playfully! The activities in this chapter help your child pay close attention to the sensation of their body when it is moving. By engaging in mindful movement activities, young children can learn how movement can bring feelings of joy, as well as calm and peace.

BLAST OFF

This activity helps children move energy through their entire body. By using large muscles in our body, we bring more oxygen to our brain so that we can better focus and experience calm. This activity can be used while waiting in line at the store or before having to sit for long periods of time.

MATERIALS:

NONE

STEPS:

1. Start by telling your child that they are going to use all of their body energy to blast off like a rocket.

2. Have your child stand with their hands straight down at their side. Have them shrug their shoulders up and down while counting 1-2-3.

3. Next have your little one shoot their hands straight up to the sky like rockets directly above their head three times.

4. Now have them squat down and touch the ground, then pop straight up, reaching their hands to the sky and saying "blast off!" Repeat three times.

5. Put it all together. Have your child shrug, reach for the sky, then squat and blast off—three times in a row.

GET CREATIVE: Alternate between fast and slow blastoffs. You can also alternate counting up to or down from 3, 5, or 10.

ANIMAL MOVES

Children get to use their imagination to move like their favorite animals, bringing awareness to different body parts and exploring how it feels to move like those animals.

STEPS:

1. Create a list of animals that your child is familiar with. Young children often can identify with large animals, such as an elephant, lion, giraffe, gorilla, dolphin, etc.

2. Have your child sit or stand. Pick an animal and have them move their body like the animal. For example, when moving like an elephant, your child would bend over, sway one arm in front like a trunk, and move slowly with heavy feet.

3. As your child moves, be sure to help bring awareness to how their body looks and feels.

GET CREATIVE: Come up with animal themes for the movements. For example, think of three to five animals that live in the ocean, desert, jungle, etc.

MATERIALS:

NONE

COUNT THE RHYTHM

This activity combines movement with sounds to engage several areas of the brain. Simply count the beats or play a familiar tune and listen. The rhythmic patterning of the movements helps engage your child's brain to build focus.

MATERIALS:

OPTIONAL: EMPTY CONTAINER AND WOODEN SPOON OR STICK

STEPS:

1. Have your child take steps around the room as you count to three or five. Keep repeating the numbers a few more times.

2. When your child is ready, add a movement to one of the numbers. For example, one, two—then jump—three. Repeat this a few more times.

3. Continue to add movement to the beats, such as jump, hop, crawl, tiptoe, twirl, etc.

4. You can also use an empty container and wooden spoon or stick to sound the beats.

AGE ADAPTATION: Two-year-olds can handle one movement to a three-count beat, while five-year-olds can handle three different movements to a five-count beat.

ROCK TO THE BEAT

Rocking, twirling, and swinging your body provides a rhythmic form of movement that stimulates the vestibular (inner ear) system. It is both energizing and calming for young children. While this activity uses rocking, you can also perform this activity at a playground swing.

STEPS:

1. Ask your child to sit on the floor.

2. Play or sing a familiar song and have your child pretend that they are in a rocking chair.

3. Have your child rock their body back and forth to the beats.

4. Experiment with other rocking movements, including side to side, on knees, on hands and knees, or standing up.

CO-REGULATION: You can also rock or twirl your child in your arms. This allows them to have the sensation of the rocking while also building a positive bond with you.

MATERIALS:

FAMILIAR SONG

HEARTBEAT DANCE

The heart is the center of our body and can beat over a hundred times per minute when we're moving, creating our body's own rhythm. Helping young children bring awareness to how their heart beats can help them achieve calm in later chapters of life. Pairing this activity with laughter also increases feelings of joy and peace.

MATERIALS:

MUSICAL SONG

OPTIONAL: STETHOSCOPE
(PLAY OR REAL)

STEPS:

1. Have your child stand where there is plenty of room to move.

2. Play music and have your child dance to the music. Play a song that brings smiles and laughter.

3. When the song is over, have your child place their hand over their heart (or use a stethoscope) and feel their heartbeat. Bring awareness to how fast your child's heart is beating and where else they may feel their heart beating, like their hands or head.

4. Try to raise or lower their heartbeat by dancing fast or slow.

CO-REGULATION: When your child is upset or scared, have them feel their heartbeat. You can help them calm down by centering their breath until their heart rate decreases.

BUG SHAKE

Using imagination and large body movements, pretend that a giant bug is on your child's body and they have to shake it off. This will bring awareness to individual parts of the body, and it's a great activity to use when waiting in line or in the car.

STEPS:

1. Your child can sit or stand where there is room to move.

2. Ask your little one to think of a type of bug and choose a body part.

3. Pretend that the bug just landed or crawled on that body part. Have your child shake that part until the bug is gone.

4. Bring awareness to what the bug feels like, such as slimy, tickly, or smooth.

SIMPLE SWAP: If your child does not like bugs, have them imagine that part of their body is being touched by a feather instead.

MATERIALS:

NONE

3

Fun with the Five Senses

Young children are innately curious and love to explore. This chapter helps them bring awareness to their five senses by deliberately focusing attention on scents, sounds, visual images, and other sensory details. When we train our brain in deliberate focus, we activate the sensory data filter which increases the thinking and purposeful parts of our brain. This enhances memory, problem-solving, relationships, creativity, and physical performance.

GUESS THE SOUND

This activity helps children notice the sounds around them, which will build their ability to focus their attention and inhibit responses to things we are trying to ignore.

MATERIALS:
NONE

STEPS:

1. Your child can either sit or lie down inside or outside.

2. Have your little one quiet their body and listen to the sounds around them. They might hear the hum of the refrigerator or the chirping of birds.

3. When they hear a sound, they should try to identify the sound and then listen for more.

GET CREATIVE: Create a list of sounds that your child might hear, and then have them check each sound off the list as they identify them.

MAGIC WATER

Using the sense of sight, children will purposefully observe an object and bring awareness to what is happening. This activity helps young children slow down and focus their attention on a visual object; it also increases their language as they describe what they see and feel.

STEPS:

1. Fill a clear container with warm water and place it in front of your child.

2. Drop at least six drops of food dye into the container.

3. Watch carefully with your child, observing together what is happening. Ask them to describe what they see as the color moves through the water.

4. Have fun mixing colors, or replace the water as you explore different hues.

SIMPLE SWAP: Put other items that will release colors—such as colorful candy, paint, or old markers—in the water and see what happens.

MATERIALS:

WARM WATER

LARGE CLEAR CONTAINER (E.G., GALLON WATER JUG, LARGE BOWL)

FOOD COLORING

CLOUD WATCHING

Young children can sharpen their visual discrimination skills with this activity, which can start to help your child distinguish between different symbols, like shapes, letters, and numbers.

MATERIALS:
OPTIONAL: BLANKET
TO LIE ON

STEPS:

1. When clouds are visible, lie on your back or sit down outside next to your child.

2. Ask your child to look for shapes or animals in the clouds.

3. Have them describe to you what they see, watching as the clouds turn into other objects.

GET CREATIVE: For a rainy day, use flashlights and every-day items to create shadows on the wall.

MYSTERY SCENTS

Smells activate parts of our brain that are tied to our emotions and memory. This activity helps young children experience several distinct aromas and gain an impression of them. Although most young children will have a strong reaction one way or another, this helps them pause before they decide.

STEPS:

1. Place the scent samples in containers (for liquid scents, saturate a cotton ball).

2. Have your child sniff the smell for several seconds without reacting.

3. Ask them to describe what they smell and tell you if they find the aroma pleasant or not.

CO-REGULATION: Create a list of scents that your child finds calming. Before bed, or when they are having a hard time, have them smell the scents to provide a relaxing experience.

MATERIALS:

SMALL CONTAINERS WITH LIDS (E.G., SMALL WATER BOTTLES, CLEANED SPICE JARS, EMPTY PILL BOTTLES)

4 OR 5 FAMILIAR SCENTS (E.G., BABY POWDER, VINEGAR, VANILLA, CINNAMON, COFFEE, ORANGE JUICE)

MINDFUL EATING

Most young children have a hard time sitting still to eat. While this mealtime restlessness is age appropriate, this activity can help gently guide mindful awareness to eating. Remember to keep the activity fun and let your child explore different tastes and textures. With practice, this activity could help your child be more open to trying new foods.

MATERIALS:

SMALL BITES OF
FOOD (E.G., PRETZELS,
MARSHMALLOWS,
ORANGES, YOGURT)

STEPS:

1. Place small bites of food in front of your child. You can present one at a time or offer a selection. Be sure that whatever bites you use for this activity are age-appropriate and safe from choking hazards.

2. Distinguish this activity from mealtime by having your child explore the food. Have them pick it up, look at it, or smell it.

3. Your child should then slowly chew the food, but ask them not to swallow it yet. Instead, have them chew it 5 to 10 times. You can count out loud to help them.

4. Ask them to swallow the food and then describe how it tasted.

SIMPLE SWAP: Some children will not like certain textures or colors. Explore with them why they don't like something, but be sure that this activity is fun—with no consequences for their preferences.

FUN WITH FINGERS

Young children love to explore with their hands. This activity uses soft textures like shaving cream or play dough to explore our sense of touch. Activating the nervous system in our hands provides stimulation in our brain that both excites and calms.

STEPS:

1. Put a plastic tablecloth on the table or use an easy to clean surface.

2. Cover part of the area with shaving cream or play dough.

3. Have your child use one or more fingers to explore the material.

4. Ask them to describe how it feels and notice any change the more they play with it.

SIMPLE SWAP: If your child does not like the feel of the materials, place them in a sealable storage bag. Your little one can still get the squishy feeling without having to touch the materials.

MATERIALS:

SOFT TEXTURES (E.G., SHAVING CREAM, PLAY DOUGH, SLIME)

EASY TO CLEAN SURFACE OR TABLE COVERING

4
Adventures in Feelings

Young children experience many feelings—but expressing those feelings is not always easy. Instead, they often rely on their actions to let you know how they feel. Yet children as young as two can begin to identify and verbalize how they are feeling. Most feeling identification at that age begins with four basic feelings: happy, sad, scared, and mad. These emotions are often automatic and can easily be seen in facial and body postures. Once children have mastered these, they can move on to other feelings, like joyful, bored, worried, and frustrated.

The activities in this chapter help you explore these feelings with your child. Mindfulness practices help children experience feelings by recognizing and naming them without judgment.

MIRROR FACES

Young children love to look at faces, so help them notice the clues in facial expressions that signify basic emotions like happy, sad, scared, and mad. This activity also helps build empathy for others by teaching how others feel.

MATERIALS:
MIRROR (EITHER HANDHELD OR FULL-LENGTH)

STEPS:

1. Have your child face the mirror.

2. Suggest emotions, such as happy, sad, scared, and mad, asking your child to express the emotion on their face.

3. Optional: Highlight the position of facial features, such as eyebrows, eyes, and mouth. For example, happy shows eyebrows relaxed, eyes open, and mouth smiling.

GET CREATIVE: Sit face-to-face with your child and model an emotion, and then have your child guess the emotion while copying your facial expression.

DEEP BREATH HUG

Young children can experience strong emotions, which can be overwhelming for them. This activity teaches a mindful way to handle those strong feelings without judgment through a deep breath hug. As you model the deep breathing, your child will naturally follow suit and learn to regulate their feelings.

STEPS:

1. The next time your child is upset, needs comfort, or simply wants a connection with you, ask if they need a hug.

2. If they say no, wait for them to be ready. You might need to ask again in a few minutes.

3. Once your child is ready, embrace them and start taking deep breaths, in through your nose and out through your mouth. If your child is crying, exaggerate the sounds so that they can hear your breathing.

4. As your child starts breathing with you, take three to five additional deep breaths together.

5. While breathing, relax any muscles that feel tight and let go of any of the tension you may feel. Let your mind clear and focus on the rhythmic sounds of the breathing.

MATERIALS:

NONE

CO-REGULATION: Use this with your whole family at the start or end of the day. It is a great way to say good morning or good night.

FEELINGS WALK

This will assist your child in building awareness of how things around them make them feel. Some children attach colors or textures to different emotions, which can help build their feelings vocabulary in a fun way.

MATERIALS:

NONE

STEPS:

1. While on a walk, ask your child about the things around them and how they make them feel.

2. Feel free to model this for them ("I see a flower that makes me feel happy").

3. You can also go on a feelings scavenger hunt by finding all the things that make your child experience a certain emotion (e.g., kind, peaceful, loved, pleased, friendly).

4. In addition, you can print out a feelings chart online and see how many feelings you both can find on the walk.

AGE ADAPTATION: Two-year-olds should begin with the four core feelings: happy, sad, scared, and mad. As your child becomes more proficient at identifying and expressing these feelings, you can expand their feelings vocabulary. See the resource section on page 53 for links to feelings charts.

MAKING FACES

Understanding feelings allows your child to build ways to express how they are experiencing the world around them. This activity invites your child to draw feeling faces on paper plates—a great way to help your child role play different emotions.

STEPS:

1. Spread out the paper plates and art materials, and then begin with one feeling word, such as happy.

2. Ask your child to draw a happy face on the paper plate. Feel free to help if needed.

3. Decorate the face with embellishments, such as hair or jewelry.

4. Describe different scenarios for your child, or ask them to describe them for you, and select which feeling face they would make.

MATERIALS:

2 TO 5 PAPER PLATES

DRAWING MATERIALS, SUCH AS CRAYONS, MARKERS, OR COLORED PENCILS

AGE ADAPTATION: Two-year-olds may only be able to distinguish the four basic feelings: happy, sad, scared, and mad. Older children should be able to focus on other facial features, like eyebrows, to help distinguish mad from disappointed, for example.

PEACE WAND

This handmade item is held when someone wants to talk; it can help young children build a way to use their words to express emotions to others, learning how to be mindful of thoughts, feelings, and words.

MATERIALS:

LARGE CRAFT, PAINT, OR TREE STICK

WATER-BASED PAINTS

DECORATING ITEMS, SUCH AS SEQUINS, GLITTER, FELT, BUTTONS, ETC.

CRAFT GLUE

INDEX CARD (OPTIONAL)

STEPS:

1. Gather your supplies and then decorate the wand in a way that is peaceful, such as using hearts or waves.

2. Model how to use the peace wand. Tell your child that when they are upset, they can notice how their body feels. For example, their hands might feel tight, their head might be hot or racing, or their feet might feel like moving.

3. Your child should get the wand whenever they are feeling upset and want to talk it out with you or another family member. Once the other person accepts the peace talk, they should stop what they are doing and place the wand between them.

4. Each should then take turns holding the wand and telling the other person how they feel and what would help them feel better.

AGE ADAPTATION: If your child needs help finding the right words, you can write on an index card "I feel _____ when _____. I need _____."

BUBBLE FUN

Laughter is the best way to boost the happy chemicals in our brain—and what is more fun than bubbles?! And when you do this with your child, you get the same benefit by watching their laughter and joining in.

STEPS:

1. Your child can stand or sit within your arms reach.

2. Start to blow the bubbles and ask your child to pop them.

3. Encourage your child to really look at the bubbles, noticing how they change colors, float, or sink fast.

MATERIALS:

BUBBLES

GET CREATIVE: If you don't have any bubbles, **make** them with your child. Just stir together one part **dish** soap to three parts water, plus a few teaspoons of **sugar**; for your bubble wand use anything with a hole (such as a straw), or make a circular bubble wand out of pipe cleaners.

5

I Care, You Care, We Care

Babies are born completely dependent on others for their care. As they grow into toddlers and young children, they begin to learn how to exist among others. Mindfulness practices can encourage young children to expand their awareness by understanding the perspective of others and recognizing how to care for others. The activities in this chapter will help them celebrate the positive feelings of peace, gratitude, kindness, and optimism.

KINDNESS BRACELET

Social acts of kindness cultivate shared happiness, build relationships, and give us a sense of a connection to our community. Young children happen to be really good at acts of kindness, which can build their sense of compassion and empathy for others.

MATERIALS:

STRING OR PIPE CLEANER

BEADS OR ROUND
CEREAL PIECES
(E.G., TOASTED OATS)

STEPS:

1. Ask your child to name some kind things that they can do for others, such as saying please and thank you, holding the door open for others, or smiling.

2. Start to make the kindness bracelet, having your child put the beads or cereal pieces on the string or pipe cleaner. Fasten the ends together and put it on your child.

3. Whenever you see your child doing something kind, be sure to give a lot of positive reinforcement. Remind them that the bracelet represents their kindness, and that you are proud of them.

CO-REGULATION: Model acts of kindness throughout the day.

FRIENDSHIP WISH

As young children become more involved in social activities, they begin to understand what it means to be a friend. This activity helps your child celebrate their friendships by creating wishes that they have for those relationships. This is also a great way to send happy thoughts to family or friends they do not see every day.

STEPS:

1. Sit with your child at a table or on the floor.

2. Tell them to think about one or two of their friends. They can be peers, siblings, pets, or even imaginary friends.

3. Have them draw or write about something they wish for each friend. For example, they can wish that the dog gets a special treat.

4. Post the friendship wish so that your child can see all the kind things they have wished for others.

5. Optional: Complete one a day for family or friends or send them in the mail.

MATERIALS:

PAPER, ANY COLOR THEY WISH

DRAWING MATERIALS, SUCH AS CRAYONS, MARKERS, OR COLORED PENCILS

AGE ADAPTATION: Young toddlers may be just beginning to use writing tools. Instead of writing, you can find pictures in magazines or print out online images, then have them glue the photos to the paper.

HEARTFELT THOUGHTS

Understanding other perspectives helps build compassion. This activity allows a child to learn caring thoughts about other people or things, encouraging them to focus on positive thoughts when something is happening that is beyond their control. It is meant to be done in the moment and repeated whenever needed.

MATERIALS:

A SPECIFIC PLACE TO TALLY THE HEARTFUL THOUGHTS YOU SEND

STEPS:

1. Sit with your child and talk about some of the kind thoughts they have about others.

2. Explain that you are going to be on a special mission to send heartfelt thoughts to others. For example, if you are driving and see a young boy crying, you and your child could say a kind thing about him to each other.

3. Choose a time frame that you will do this activity, such as over the next week or month.

4. Keep count of how many heartful thoughts you can send to others.

GET CREATIVE: Find a local mission or organization that needs help or supplies. Volunteer to draw or write kind thoughts to them.

GRATEFUL WALK

Young children are natural explorers. Channeling mindfulness when exploring the outdoors—this activity focuses on gratitude—builds a deeper appreciation for the things we see every day.

STEPS:

1. While on a walk, ask your child about what they notice around them. They can either say it aloud or point to things.

2. Express your feelings for what you both see during the walk, such as "I am grateful for the flowers because they feed the bees."

3. You can also create a list of things you hope to see on the walk and go on a scavenger hunt.

MATERIALS:

NONE

SIMPLE SWAP: Don't let the rain stop you! Instead, have an indoor grateful walk by finding different things around the house and explaining why you are grateful for them. For example, "I am grateful for this blanket because it keeps me warm at night."

ANIMAL CARETAKER

Children build empathy by caring for others. One of their first experiences as a caretaker is usually with animals, real or imagined.

MATERIALS:

PINECONE OR STICK

PEANUT BUTTER OR
SUNFLOWER SEED BUTTER

BIRD SEED OR SMALL
ANIMAL FEED

OPTIONAL: STRING TO
HANG OUTSIDE

STEPS:

1. Together, think about the birds, squirrels, or other small animals in your neighborhood.

2. Tell your child that you are going to be a helper to the animals by creating something the animals can eat.

3. Spread the peanut or sunflower seed butter on the pinecone or stick.

4. Cover it with bird seed or small animal feed. Optional: Tie a string to one end to hang it.

5. Take it outside and leave it or hang it up for the animals. Have your child watch for signs that it is being enjoyed.

AGE ADAPTATION: Four- and five-year-olds may be able to complete larger supervised tasks for animals. It can be feeding or brushing your or a neighbor's pet, or taking supplies to a local animal shelter.

FORGIVENESS MATTERS

Learning how to forgive takes purposeful action, and practicing this act will help kids find their confidence so they can forgive themselves and others when mistakes are made.

STEPS:

1. Sit or stand across from your child. Explain that everyone makes mistakes, and these mistakes are not bad but rather something we can learn from.

2. Both of you should take a spoon. Tell your child that you are going to pass the egg (or another small item) back and forth with it.

3. Try not to drop it, but let your child know that if they do, it is okay. You can simply say, "Oops" or "Sorry," and the other will respond with "That's okay" or "I forgive you."

4. Begin to pass the egg back and forth, counting the number of times passed. You can also use a timer when your child gets good at the game.

5. Ask your child to reflect on how it felt when they were able to pass the egg or when it dropped. Remind them that all those feelings are okay.

MATERIALS:

ONE SPOON
PER PERSON/CHILD

PLASTIC EGG OR SMALL
ITEM THAT WILL FIT ON
THE SPOON

OPTIONAL: TIMER

GET CREATIVE: Not all children like to say sorry. Instead of letting it turn into a power struggle, have your child come up with different phrases to say when they make a mistake.

6
Winding Down Time

Learning to calm down can be hard for young children. Often, they will move around until they literally collapse on the floor. Luckily, you *can* teach your child how to calm their body and brain throughout the day with activities that are still fun to do.

CALMING BOTTLE

This water bottle filled with glitter or other materials creates a fun sensory experience that allows your child to calm and center themselves throughout the day.

MATERIALS:

1 (12- TO 20-OUNCE) , CLEAR PLASTIC DRINK BOTTLE, EMPTY AND CLEAN .

FUNNEL (OPTIONAL)

WARM WATER

CLEAR SCHOOL GLUE

FILLINGS LIKE GLITTER, BEADS, SEQUINS, ETC.

LIQUID FOOD COLORING (OPTIONAL)

PERMANENT GLUE

STEPS:

1. With your child, fill the bottle about one-third of the way with warm water, using a funnel if needed.

2. Add about another one-third of clear school glue to the bottle.

3. Have your child add any additional items they would like to the bottle.

4. Fill the bottle the rest of the way with warm water.

5. Add permanent glue to the threads on the inner part of the lid and seal it tightly onto the bottle.

6. Have your child experiment with the bottle by shaking it and then watching how the contents move.

GET CREATIVE: Create colored bottles for the four categories of feelings, such as yellow for happy, blue for sad, purple for scared, and red for mad. Your child can then identify their feelings by choosing the sensory bottle that corresponds with how they are feeling.

SLOW SIT-UP

This activity can teach children how to focus on small movements, slowing down their bodies and feeling the different parts move in purposeful ways. This is a great way to help a child get out some energy before sitting in the car or at the table.

STEPS:

1. Ask your child to lie on the floor faceup.

2. Tell them to first lift only their head, then shoulders, chest, and stomach until they are in a sitting position.

3. Begin again.

MATERIALS:
NONE

GET CREATIVE: Alternate between fast and slow sit-ups. Use different arm positions: First have their arms start above their head, then straight out in front. Ask your child to come up with variations.

BELLY BUDDIES

This is great for helping your little one calm down before bed.

MATERIALS:

STUFFED ANIMAL

STEPS:

1. Ask your child to lay on the floor or bed faceup.

2. Place a stuffed animal or other favorite item on their belly.

3. Tell them to breathe in silence and notice how their belly buddy moves up and down.

4. Prompt them to imagine any other sensations and thoughts that come to mind.

5. Continue to watch the belly buddy as your child breathes in and out.

CO-REGULATION: When you are feeling upset, model for your child how you can use deep breathing to calm yourself.

COTTON BALL BREATHING

Help your child control their breathing in a fun way—all you need are a few cotton balls!

STEPS:

1. Sit with your child on the floor or at a table.

2. Give them a cotton ball, asking them to place it either on the table or in their palm.

3. Have them gently blow the cotton ball so that it slowly moves across the table or their palm.

4. If it falls off, just try again.

MATERIALS:
2 OR 3 COTTON BALLS

SIMPLE SWAP: No cotton balls? No problem! Simply use anything that is lightweight, such as craft poms, popcorn, or tissue.

LOOK IN THE MIRROR

Children can visualize their breath simply by staring in the mirror.

MATERIALS:

MIRROR (EITHER
HANDHELD
OR FULL-LENGTH)

PAPER TOWEL OR TISSUE

STEPS:

1. Your child should sit next to a mirror or hold one in their hand.

2. Tell your child to pretend to be a dragon (or unicorn) and blow on the mirror.

3. Start off with slow breaths, allowing your child to notice when steam forms on the mirror.

4. Practice to see how much of the mirror can fill up with steam, blowing soft and hard to see how foggy it gets.

SIMPLE SWAP: Your child can also use a window or glass tabletop to practice breathing. Just be careful letting your child do this if it drives you nuts to see fingerprints or smudges on glass!

BODY SQUEEZE

Your little one can use this task to relax their whole body—a great way to calm before a nap or bedtime.

STEPS:

1. Make sure your child is lying in a comfortable position.

2. Explain that they are going to use their mind to tense and relax muscles.

3. When your child is ready, begin with muscles in or near the feet and tell them to tense a muscle and hold it for three seconds before relaxing it.

4. Young children may do just the large muscles (e.g., legs, stomach, arms, shoulders, head), while older children can work on adding smaller muscles (e.g., toes, calf, thigh, biceps, fingers, forehead).

5. Continue all the way up until reaching the head. Have your child reflect on how the activity made them feel.

CO-REGULATION: If your child is upset, you can gently give squeezes all the way up your child's body. This type of deep pressure can be very relaxing to the brain and body.

MATERIALS:

NONE

RESOURCES

Websites

Zero to Three: *www.zerotothree.org/resources/2268-mindfulness-for-parents*
    This early childhood website has a variety of resources on mindfulness for toddlers and young children.

Mindful: *www.mindful.org*
    A great place for anyone wanting to learn more about mindfulness, this website has resources on finding a community, gaining insight, exploring information, and getting inspiration to help live more mindfully. They also publish a print and digital magazine called *Mindful*.

Teaching Children Meditation: *www.teachchildrenmeditation.com/meditation-for-toddlers*
    A good place for resources on how to teach kids mindfulness and meditation, this organization offers training for educators and professionals to become a certified Kids Meditation Teacher. In addition, there is information about working with children with autism, ADHD, trauma, and other special educational needs.

Reward Charts 4 Kids: *www.rewardcharts4kids.com/feelings-chart*
    This website offers free printable feelings and mood charts for a variety of contexts.

Books for Kids

Crab and Whale by Christiane Kerr and Mark Pallis. Ages 2 to 11 years. This book is designed to gently introduce kids to the practice of mindfulness, touching on the values of acceptance, generosity, gratitude, kindness, patience, and trust.

How Kind! by Mary Murphy. Ages 2 to 5 years. This book is a great way to introduce kindness to toddlers and young children through a story about how all the animals are kind to each other.

Puppy Mind by Andrew Jordan Nance. Ages 3 to 7 years. *Puppy Mind* is a delightful story about how our mind sometimes wanders but we can train it to be more in the present.

Books for Parents

Awakening Joy for Kids: A Hands-On Guide for Grown-Ups to Nourish Themselves and Raise Mindful, Happy Children by James Baraz and Michele Lilyanna. This is a guide for caregivers and children to find ways to explore joy in each day together.

Breathe, Mama, Breathe: 5-Minute Mindfulness for Busy Moms by Shonda Moralis. This book boasts five minutes of daily meditation that can teach every parent to become more mindful.

Ready, Set, Breathe: Practicing Mindfulness with Your Children for Fewer Meltdowns and a More Peaceful Family by Carla Naumburg. Offering practical solutions, this book helps you and your child use mindfulness to navigate challenges and meltdowns.

REFERENCES

Kabat-Zinn, Jon. *Wherever You Go, There You Are: Mindfulness Meditation in Everyday Life.* New York, NY: Hyperion, 1994.

Murray, Desiree W., Katie Rosanbalm, Christina Christopoulos, and Amar Hamoudi. *Self-Regulation and Toxic Stress: Foundations for Understanding Self-Regulation from an Applied Developmental Perspective* (OPRE Report # 2015-21). Washington, DC: Office of Planning, Research and Evaluation, Administration for Children and Families, U.S. Department of Health and Human Services, January 2015. https://fpg.unc.edu/node/7587.

INDEX

ACKNOWLEDGMENTS

This book could not be written without the Southeast Alternative School; the fellow educators who work tirelessly each day to accept and love each student who walks in the door, just as they are; and the students who are brave enough to share their struggles with the adults on their journey. You all are loved just as you are!

ABOUT THE AUTHOR

Hiedi France, EdD, is a mother of two wonderful teenagers and a school psychologist who has devoted her career to helping children succeed. She holds three degrees: a BS in Psychology from Northern Illinois University, an MEd in School Psychology from Loyola University, and her doctorate, an EdD in educational leadership from Lewis University focusing on social justice. Dr. France has worked with students with mental health needs in the education system for 18 years, applying her studies of education and psychology to support the social-emotional and psychological needs of students in order for them to succeed and be the best versions of themselves. She is also the founder of Behavior Savers (BehaviorSavers.com) which creates easy-to-use social-emotional resources for educators.

CPSIA information can be obtained
at www.ICGtesting.com
Printed in the USA
JSHW021813210620
6291JS00003B/54